Sea of Tears to Purify Your Soul: Based on the Teaching of Ibn Qayyim and Ibn Jawzi

Omer Sulayman

Introduction

How many times have we crossed the line and broken through the door of Allah's prohibition? We all must have a similar answer: "I can't count my turning away from Him."

Dear reader!

Every one requires to read this great book by the esteemed scholar. These sins and negligence of ours is truly saddening and should be pondered upon. After all, every obedience and disobedience are recorded by Him, no matter how small. And, He will hold us accountable for every act of disobedience. Unfortunately, we don't always realize the danger of this negligence. We continue to get carried away, complacent, and oblivious to the fact that we will be held accountable.

We often procrastinate on the deeds that will save us on the Day of Resurrection. We are not deterred by the world and its games of lust. We neglect to develop the habit of asking for forgiveness and establishing an intimate relationship with Allah.

Sometimes we realize, what's the point of pursuing wealth if we end up leaving it behind. We realize that we have to word hard to earn the minimum *halal* wealth required to lead a good life such that we are able to pray and feed our families, and to avoid hunger and poverty. However, this realization fades away in the whirlwind of our busy lives.

This realization is often suppressed by our interpretation of our responsibilities to family, humanity, and others. We are again more dexterous in seeking the world, and doing sins to earn more that the wealth that we require, and mostly we earn such wealth through *haram* ways, as if the desire to seek wealth is never-ending. Meanwhile, when looking for the hereafter, which has eternal value, we are sluggish. Let's reflect! In the past month, how many nights have you spent chasing the world and how many nights have you spent in the Hereafter?

This book reminds us all how life in this world is temporary. In fact, this transience determines the eternity of the next stage of our journey. Therefore, this book demands that you put aside worldly matters before you read it. This is because only you and Allah are discussed. This narrowing of focus is important so that we quickly realize that life is actually a very personal journey from the world to the grave.

Our journey is still very long. All that we build and build in the world will not be a provision, unless it is worth goodness for others and bears fruit in taking us closer to Allah. So, it is wretched for us to only collect a little provision for this very far journey.

This book invites us to present ourselves to Allah and fill the rest of our lives with various obedience to the commands of Allah. It greets every servant who feels they have a stained record of deeds and helps them clean it with tears. Going through this book is like entering an assembly of cries of forgiveness, and having the inner experience of the people of who wake up in the night to pray to Allah.

This work was written by a very authoritative scholar of his time, Imam Abu al-Faraj 'Abd Rahman ibn 'Ali al-Jawzî (Allah have mercy on him). He was born in the fifth century A.H. and was a descendant of the first caliph, Abû Bakr (Allah be pleased with him). At a young age (10 years old), he was already a scholar. He was classified as a prolific scholar (writing more than 300 works) and mastered many disciplines (ulum Quran, ulum hadith, Fiqh, Usul fiqh, history, biography, and da'wah). He was known to be intelligent, strong in argument, and courageous in defending the truth. He was also very much far away from *haram* objects and limited himself in worldly pleasures.

Having applied this teaching himself in his daily life, it is only fitting that Ibn al-Jawzî constantly invites us to sell the world for our hereafter. He also ensures that it is by prioritizing the hereafter that we will be fortunate in the world. He says, "The hardships of this world will not harm you if you have a store of the goodness of the hereafter. But if you ride it (the world), it will carry you. And, if you carry it, it will make you perish."

Many verses, hadiths, and poems that Ibn al-Jawzî presents ignite our desire to repent. There are also many stories about the companions of the Prophet and the close friends of Allah (the scholars of Islam who follow the Quran and authentic Hadeeth and are upon the way of the Salaf and Ahle-Hadeeth). These stories tell a variety of experiences, realizations, and wisdom that we can emulate or learn from in becoming a better person. The last five chapters of the book even contain signs of attitudes and actions that we should do and avoid as Muslims: keeping the tongue moving for the sake of Allah, abandoning useless talk, stop looking for disgrace and digging up other people's ugliness, do not commit adultery, do not complain, do not gossip, and so on.

If you intend to renounce evil and sin, feel that you often indulge in lust, become a prisoner of the world and a slave to lust, then this book can be the right companion to become a better Muslim. Ibn al-Jawzi emphasizes that the dowry of the hereafter is actually simple: a sincere heart and a reciting tongue. So, reading this book should be accompanied by the realization that the repentant's entire time is filled with charity: speaking while remembering Him, moving with His commands, grieving because of His reprimands, and rejoicing because of being close to Him.

You will find many extreme stories in this book. For example, the man who at the end of his life asked: "Put my cheek on the ground and step on it so that I may feel the humiliation of this world and the pleasure of being with Allah." Or, the person who cried in repentance until he fainted, then died. Against such stories, perhaps it is not wise to judge them based on our experience of this world of ours where everyone is seeking wealth and indulging in sins. We should take a positive perspective so that we can still explore Ibn al-Jawzî's wisdom. For example:

1. This book written by a classical scholar is still referred to by many modern Muslim writers.

The book also views death as a gateway to the next stage of the human journey. So it is natural and even interesting if the story of the plea for forgiveness in this book is often attached to the background of the death of the perpetrators.

Ibn al-Jawzî's style of speech also feels wise because he often uses stories instead of dictating to us.

2. The audience for this book is the people of the fifth century AH who have different experiences and knowledge from us. We need to imagine ourselves living at the time of the book's writing in order to absorb its basic message. Isn't the essence of foolishness that it doesn't recognize the times and the details of the world around it?

3. Regardless of the weakness of the transmission, these stories perhaps show how the energy of repentance so often reveals the human closeness to the All-Forgiving.

4. And, other points of view that have the perspective of good prejudice: Who knows, the treasures of repentance come to us in a different form than what we imagine?

Another thing we need to take away from this book is that it seems to say that the fastest way to reach closeness to Allah is to repent.

1

O captive of the world, O slave of lust, O den of sin, O receptacle of calamity, remember what you have done and fear Allah! Let Him not see your wrongdoing and disobedience, so that He bars you from His door, He keeps you away from His side, and He prevents you from being close with His friends. If so, you fall into the abyss of disgrace and are caught in the net of loss. Whenever you want to free yourself from misguidance, the voice of Allah calls out:

Turn away from Us, you do not come near Us, O traitor who neglects Us.

You turned away from Us and did not obey Us

You want to seek Our pleasure, while the relationship has been broken

How do you now want to approach Us

while for a long time you have forgotten Us O breaker of promises, no one is connected to Us except the one who strives himself in Our way and who truly humbles himself.

O buyer of perishable goods with something eternal, do you not feel a loss?

How sweet are the days of meeting and how bitter the days of separation.

The life of a people does not become good except by emigrating, staying up late while reading the Qur'an, and passing the night standing before and prostrating to God.

'Abd al-'Azîz ibn Salmân al-'Abid relates the story of a man who purified himself and wept for sixty years because he longed for Allah:

I dreamed that I was on the banks of a river of very fragrant musk water. The pearl trees were on its banks, the mud was amber oil, and the water was very fragrant. On the banks of the river, beautiful maidens were chanting, "Glory to Allah and Most High. Glory be to Him. Glory to the One Who is sanctified by every tongue. Glory be to the One who is the Eternal of all times. We are creatures of the Glorious Compassionate One. We are immortal and will not die forever. We are always pleased and never angry. We are favors that will never change." I asked, "Who are you?" They replied, "We are the creatures of Allah." I asked, "What are you doing here?" They gave a beautiful answer in unison:
The Lord of mankind, the Sustainer of Muhammad (peace and blessings of Allah be upon him), provided us for the people who rise up to worship in the darkness of the night (pray Tahajjud – the night prayer along with all the other compulsory acts of worship such as the five prayers, and also those who keep themselves away from grave worship, sins, and Bidaah – the newly innovated things in the religion of Allah).

They pray to their Lord, *Rabbul-alamin*. They rise when others are fast asleep.

"Well, well," I said, "who, then, are the people to whom Allah has given happiness?" They asked back, "Don't you know?" "No, by Allah," I replied. They continued, "They are the people who worship fervently at night and stay up late with the Quran."

The Prophet (peace and blessings of Allah be upon him) said, "If a person commits a sin and truly repents to Allah, He accepts every good deed he has done and forgives every sin he ever committed, and raises for him a degree in Paradise for every good action, and Allah gives him a palace in Paradise for every good deed. Allah will marry him to one of the beautiful virgins."

The Messenger of Allah (peace and blessings of Allah be upon him) also said:

Allah revealed to Dâwûd (peace be upon him), "O Dâwûd, give glad tidings to the sinners and warn the righteous!" Prophet Dâwûd (peace be upon him) was astonished and asked, "O Lord, how shall I give glad tidings to the sinners and warnings to the righteous?" Allah said, "O Dâwûd, give glad tidings to the sinners that there is no sin that I cannot forgive and warn the righteous not to be proud of their deeds. When I punish someone, he will surely perish. O Dawud, if you confess your love for Me, then remove the love for the world from your heart. Love for Me and love for the world cannot come together in one heart. O Dâwûd, whoever loves Me, he will certainly make *Tahajjud* (the night *tarawih witr* prayer) before Me when others sleep. (He will) remember Me in seclusion when others are negligent, and be grateful for My favors when others forget Me."

Blessed is the person who, when his eyes are awake at night

He passes the night anxious for the love of his Lord

He rises alone to gaze at the stars out of longing for Him

while God's eyes look lovingly upon him.

The Prophet (peace and blessings of Allah be upon him) said, "Goodness (righteousness) does not vanish and sins are not forgotten. The Almighty is not mortal (He is ever living). Do as you please, for you will be rewarded according to your deeds (you will be judged)."

O my brother, do you know what you have done? You have bought the far by selling the near, bought lust by selling reason, and bought the world by selling religion.

Arise and weep for yourself. Always weep to please Him.

When a young man fears Allah in all his desires, he is perfect.

Jâbir ibn 'Abd Allâh (Allah be pleased with him) narrated that the Messenger of Allah (peace and blessings of Allah be upon him) said, "Allah does not remove a servant from committing sins unless He wants to grant him forgiveness and Allah does not make a servant happy in doing good deeds unless He wants to receive good from him (accept his good actions)."

'Abdullah ibn 'Abbâs (Allah be pleased with him) narrated that the Prophet (peace and blessings of Allah be upon him) said, "When they come out of the grave, the bodies of the repentant emit the fragrance of musk. They receive a table from Paradise and eat from it under the shade of the Throne, while other people are at the door of accountability."

It is narrated that a man came to the Messenger of Allah (peace be upon him) and said, "O Messenger of Allah, with what can I guard myself from Hell?" He replied, "With your tears." "How?" the man asked. He (peace be upon him) explained, "Shed tears out of fear of Allah, for the eyes that weep out of fear of Him will not be punished." (This hadith is not authentic.)

'Abd-Allah ibn Mas'ud r.a. narrated that the Messenger of Allah said:

The tears of a believer out of fear of Allah are better than the whole world and better than a year's worship. Reflecting on the greatness and power of Allah for a moment is better than fasting sixty days and praying sixty nights. Doesn't Allah have angels who call out every day and night, "O forty-year-old, the crops are about to be harvested. O you who are fifty years old, come to the reckoning. O you who are sixty years old, what are you doing? What have you done and what have you forsaken? O seventy-year-old, what are you waiting for? Oh, if only beings were not created. If only they knew what they were created for and did good deeds for it. Has not the time come? Be careful!" (the chain of transmission of this hadeeth is weak).

Clean your gray hair from dirt (sins). The white color is not fit to carry dirt.

O bad servant, how often you transgress, but I cover. How often you broke through the door of prohibition, but I repaired it. How often We tried to shed your tears of fear, but they did not come out. How often We tried to establish a relationship through obedience, but you ran away and left. How many of My favors have been bestowed upon you, yet you are ungrateful. The world and the play of lust have deceived you, while you neither hear nor see. I subjected the universe for you, but you transgress and disbelieve. You ask for eternity in the world, while it is only a bridge to cross.

They (this world and its temptations) prevented you from drinking the drink of love and sincerity when they saw you betraying and disgracing yourself.

It is narrated that al-Hasan al-Basrî r.a. said:

I met a majusi (Magian) who had resigned himself to death. He lived in front of my house. He was a good neighbor, well behaved, and had a good character. I prayed that Allah would guide him before his death and make him a Muslim. I asked him, "What are you suffering from and how are you?" He replied, "My heart is sick. My body is bad and I am helpless at all times. My grave is horrible and unpleasant. The journey is very long, and I have no provisions. The *Sirat* (bridge of hell) is so slippery, I cannot cross it. The fire is so hot, and I have no body armor. Heaven is so high, while I have no ration. God is just, while I have no excuse." I asked, "Why don't you embrace Islam to be saved?" He replied, "O Shaykh, the key is in the hand of the

Opener and the lock is here (while pointing to his chest)."
He then fainted.

Al-Hasan continued:

I prayed, "O my Lord, if this Magi man is good according
to your destiny, hasten it for him before his soul leaves the
world and his hopes are dashed." Not long after that, the
magi came to his senses and opened his eyes. He said, "O
Shaykh, God the Opener has sent the key. Stretch out your
hand! I testify that there is no God but Allah and I testify
that Muhammad is the messenger of Allah." His soul then
went out to the mercy of Allah.

Oh my trust! the foundation of my hope!

You are my hope and my helper

Cover my deeds with goodness and grant me repentance
before death

O Lord, help me.

My brothers, why sleep when you are awake?

Why doubt when you see?

Why neglect when you have testified?

Why be absent-minded when you are aware?

Why be silent when you will be prosecuted?

Why stay when the times are sure to go?

Hasn't the time come for the sleepers to wake up?

Hasn't the time come for the negligent to learn a lesson?

Know, all the people of this world are on a journey.

Therefore, do good actions for yourself so that you will be saved from hell on the Day of Resurrection.

The time has come to go, so be careful

and watch out for everything

Do not get carried away with today or tomorrow

How many people get carried away and fall into danger.

Al-Junayd said, "Al-Sari al-Saqathi r.a. was always busy in worship. He was so busy that he did not have time to repeat the recitation that he had missed."

So was 'Umar ibn al-Khattâb (Allah be pleased with him). There was no sleep for him. When he looked sleepy while sitting, someone once asked, "O Amirul-muminin (the leader of the believers), you do not sleep?" He replied, "How can I sleep? If I sleep during the day, I neglect the rights of the people, and if I sleep at night, I neglect my share from Allah."

Al-Junayd r.a. said, "I have never seen anyone more devoted to worship than al-Sarî al-Saqathî. For 78 years he did not lie down except when he died." He also said, "I heard al-Sarî al-Saqathi r.a saying, 'If it were not for Friday prayers and congregational prayers, I would not leave my house. I would have stayed at home until I died.'"

Abu Bakr al-Shaydalânî relates the story of Sulaymân ibn Manshûr ibn 'Ammâr:

I met my father in a dream. I asked him, "What did Allah do to you, Father?" He said, "God drew me near and said, 'O Old Man who has done much evil, do you know why I forgave you?' 'No, O Lord,' I replied. God explained, 'You once sat and spoke among people until they wept. Among them was My servant who wept, whereas before he had never wept out of fear of Me. For his weeping I forgave you. I forgave all the worshippers present in the assembly. You were among them.'"

'Ali ibn Muhammad ibn Ibrâhîm al-Shaffâr narrates, "One night I went to Aswad ibn Sâlim. I found him weeping as he repeatedly recited two verses of poetry:

One day I will be in the presence of God

Who questions me and reveals all.

It is enough for me (suffice me) to cross the bridge of the sword's edge with the fire blazing beneath it.

Suddenly he cried out and fainted until dawn."

It is narrated that al-Dhahhâk ibn Muzâhim said:

One night I went to the mosque of Kufa. I saw a young man prostrating himself and crying in the courtyard of the mosque. I was sure he was a close friend of Allah (worshipping Allah alone, having the belief of the Salaf, doing all the actions that He has commanded and being away from all His prohibited actions). I approached him. I heard him say:

Blessed is the man who worships You

Blessed is the man who passes the night crying out his calamities to the One Who is the Greatest.

The Greatest

There is no pain and suffering in him except love of God and longing

The servant who accepts his Lord's bounty is near, and his soul is at peace.

He continued to cry as he repeated the verse. I cried too.

Suddenly, there was a light like a flash of lightning. I immediately closed my eyes. I heard a pleasant voice, not unlike human speech, calling out from above the youth's head:

I welcome you, O My servant, and I protect you.

I have accepted all your words

Your voice is longed for by My angels

We have heard it and it is enough for you

Though the winds blow from many directions it always bows before Me.

So bow down before Me

My servant who walks in My veil Now We have forgiven your sins.

Al-Dhahhâk continued:

By God, it was the lover's speech to his Beloved. I fainted at the sight of His majesty. When I came to my senses, I heard the sound of the angels in the sky and the rumble of their wings between the sky and the earth. It seemed that the sky was very close to the earth. I saw a light that outshone the moon. The night was so full of light. I then approached him and greeted him. He answered my greeting. I said, "May Allah bless you. Who are you?" He replied, "I am Râshid ibn Sulaymân." I knew the name because I had heard it. I said, "May Allah grant you mercy. If you allow me to accompany you, I will be very happy." "No, no. Is it possible for one who enjoys worshipping Allah (alone without any partners, and asking help from Him alone) to be happy with creatures?" he said. He then left. May Allah have mercy on him.

2

O my brother, how long will you procrastinate in doing good deeds, how long will you get lost in wishful thinking, get carried away by the deadlines, and neglect the attack of death? The one who was born will return to the ground. What you build will collapse. What you gather will perish. What you do is recorded and will be questioned on the Day of Judgment...

If, when we die, we are left without resurrection then death is a rest for the living.

However, after our death we will be resurrected and questioned about everything.

It is narrated that 'Umar ibn al-Khaththâb r.a. said:

Do not be deceived by the words of Allah: "Whoever does a good deed will receive tenfold and whoever does a bad deed will receive its equivalent." Even though it is only one reward, bad deeds are accompanied by ten reprehensible things:

1. They make Allah angry, even though He is the ruler of the doer;

2. makes Satan happy

3. moves you away from Paradise;

4. takes you towards hell;

5. hurts the most beloved thing, which is yourself;

6. dirties the previously clean self;

7. disappoints the accompanying angels;

8. makes the Prophet (peace and blessings of Allah be upon him) sad in his grave;

9. witnessing the sinful self to the universe;

10. betraying all humanity and disobeying the Lord of the universe.

Dzû al-Nûn al-Misrî relates:

I once went to the Hijaz without a friend. On the way, I was stranded in the desert. My provisions were exhausted and I was about to die. It was then that a tree with low branches, drooping branches, and dense leaves appeared in the middle of the desert. I whispered to myself, "I will go to that tree to take shelter while awaiting my fate."

When I arrived near the tree and was about to take shelter in its shade, one of the branches pierced my drinking bag until all the water left in it spilled out. I felt that death was approaching. I then lay down under the tree, waiting for the Angel of Death to come. Suddenly I heard a soft voice from a sad heart: "O Lord, if this is indeed Your pleasure, increase it until You are pleased with me, O Merciful One."

I stood up and looked for the source of the voice. Suddenly I saw a handsome, well-built man lying on the sand, while a number of vultures swarmed around and pecked at his flesh. I greeted him. He answered me and said, "O Dzû al-Nûn, when the provisions are exhausted and the water is spilled, you feel that you will die and perish." I then sat near his head and wept out of pity and compassion.

Suddenly a tray of food was thrown in front of me. The man then kicked the ground with his heel and out gushed water whiter than milk and sweeter than honey. He said, "O Dzû al-Nûn, eat and drink! You must reach the House of Allah. But I have a request for you, O Dzû al-Nún. If you fulfill it, you will be rewarded and rewarded." I asked, "What is it?" He explained, "If you fulfill it, you will be rewarded. When I die, wash me and bury me so that I may be protected from wild animals and birds, then you may continue your journey. After performing the pilgrimage, you will come to the city of Baghdad and enter from the door of Zafaran. There you will find children playing. They are wearing a variety of clothes. There you will also find a young boy. All he does is remember Allah. There is a cloth wrapped around his waist and shoulders. On his face are two black lines from frequent crying. That is my son and the fruit of my heart. Give him my greetings."

Dzû al-Nûn continued:

After speaking, he said, "I testify that there is no God but Allah and I testify that Muhammad is the messenger of Allah," then breathed his last. May Allah's mercy be upon him. "Inna lillâhi wa innâ ilayhi râji'ûn," I said. I washed his body with the water, then I shrouded it with the clothes from my bag and buried it. After that, I continued my journey to the House of Allah. I performed the Hajj and then went to the Messenger of Allah (his grave in Madinah – peace and blessings of Allah be upon him). From Medina I traveled to Baghdad and arrived there on the day of the feast. I saw a number of children in different clothes playing. I looked at them and there was a child as described by the man that I met in the desert. The child was not enamored of gifts and just sat in remembrance of the One Who knows all hidden things. His countenance betrayed sadness. On his face were two black lines from frequent crying. He hummed:

All men rejoice in the feast while I rejoice in Allah the Almighty

All men adorn their garments for the feast while I am adorned with the garments of humiliation and sorrow

All men cleanse their bodies for the feast while I cleanse my heart with tears.

I greeted him. He answered my greeting and said, "Welcome, my father's messenger." I asked, "Who told you that I am your father's messenger?" He replied, "Who told me that you had buried my father in the desert. O Dzù al-Nûn, do you think you have buried my father? By Allah, my father has been taken up to *sidratulmuntaha*. Let us go to my grandmother!"

The boy took my hand and led me to his house. Arriving at the door of the house, he opened the door softly. Not long after, his grandmother came out to meet us. She looked at me and said, "Welcome, O one who has seen the face of my son." I asked, "Who told you that I had met him?" She replied, "Who told me that you have shrouded him and the shroud will be returned to you. O Dzû al-Nûn, by the greatness and majesty of God, the cloth my son is wearing is the pride of the angels in the highest realms."

The grandmother asked, "O Dzû al-Nûn, tell me how you left my son?" "I left him in the desert among the sand and rocks. He has obtained his hope from the Almighty and Forgiving God," I replied.

Upon hearing that, the grandmother embraced the child and suddenly both disappeared. I don't know whether they were taken up into the sky or swallowed by the earth. I looked for them in every corner of the house, but I couldn't find them. Suddenly a voice was heard: "O Dzû al-Nûn, do not exhaust yourself! Even the angels could not find them." "Then, where are they?" I asked. The voice replied, "The martyrs died by the sword of the polytheists, while the lovers died out of longing for Allah the Lord of the worlds. They are taken on a vehicle of light to heaven."

I then searched for my missing leather pouch. When I found it, I found that it contained the cloth in which the man's body had been wrapped, folded as before. May Allah be pleased with them and benefit us through their blessings.

3

O you who abides in sins and disobedience, disregarder of God's commands, and follower of slander and misguidance, how long are you willing to remain in evil and reluctant to draw near to God? You seek that which you will not attain from this world and how will you guard yourself against the ultimate punishment with that which you do not posses? You do not believe in Allah's guaranteed sustenance and instead disobey His commands.

O my brother, by Allah, advice no longer serves you. Events have not awakened you. The cycles of time are not felt by you and the voice of death is not heard by you. It is as if you, O poor man, are going to live forever and will never die.

By Allah, the one who atones for sins and fears hell has been fortunate and saved, while you are still busy doing wrong and sinning.

My patience is dwindling and I deserve to mourn

My heart has become unhealthy because of sin

My spirit is damaged because of sinful deeds

Gray hair announce my death

Every time I say that my heart's wounds have healed my heart is wounded again because of sin.

Fortune and favor belong only to the servant who comes to the Day of Resurrection safe and sound.

O my brother, leave this world as the pious leave it! Prepare for the death that is bound to happen! Take lessons from the passage of time and age!

O absent-minded and misguided one who is carried away by the length of the journey that Allah is delaying, but you are defiant and unafraid of the consequences of disobedience.

Al-Junayd r.a. said:

I visited al-Sari al-Saqathi when he was ill. I asked, "How are you?" He replied:

How can I complain about my condition to God when the calamity that has befallen me is from God.

I then fanned him to cool him down. Instead, he said, "How can this fan cool a chest that burns from within?" He then hummed:

This heart is burning and tears are flowing

Suffering is gathering, while patience is scattering

How can a heart that is always full of passionate longing and anxiety be calm O Lord, if there is a way out for me grant it to me as long as life remains.

It is narrated that 'Ali ibn al-Muwaffaq r.a. said, "One day I went out to call the adhan. On the way, I found a paper and put it in my sleeve. After praying, I read the paper, which turned out to read: "In the Name of Allah, the Most Merciful and the Most Compassionate. O 'Ali ibn al- Muwaffaq, do you fear poverty, when I am your Lord?!"

Al-Mazini narrated:

I met al-Shafi'i r.a. when he was sick on the eve of his death. I asked him, "How are you?" He replied, "I am about to leave this world, part with my brothers, take a sip from the glass of death, meet the bad deeds, and return to Allah. I do not know whether my soul will return to heaven where it deserves my congratulations or to hell where it deserves my condolences." He then wept and hummed:

When my heart is tight and my path is narrow only hope in Your forgiveness is my ladder

My sins seem so great but Your forgiveness,
Lord, is far greater

You always forgive sins and are kind and give *maghfirah* as a gift

If it were not for You, no servant would have survived the Satan

How could your chosen servant, Adam, have been misled by him.

O my brother, repent of sin immediately! Follow the footsteps of those who repent! Take the path of those who return to God and receive repentance and forgiveness! Exert yourself to attain the pleasure of the Merciful One! They rise up to worship in the darkness of the night and read the book of Allah.

The servants of Allah with anxious souls and trembling hearts place their foreheads on the ground and ask for their needs to the One Who sees but is not seen.

Stop at My door when calamity comes Rest assured in Me, you will surely find the best of friends.

Do not turn to other than Me, you will surely regret it

Whoever turns to other than Me will surely be disappointed.

Abû Mahfuzh Ma'ruf al-Karkhî has been honored by Allah Swt. since his childhood. His brother, 'Îsâ, narrates:

My brother Ma'ruf and I were at school. At that time we were Christians. Our teacher taught the students to mention God the Father and God the Son, but my brother, Ma'rûf, shouted: "Ahad, ahad (One, one)." Hearing this, the teacher was very angry. Ma'rûf was hit so hard that he ran away. Ma'ruf did not come back for a long time, and Ma'ruf's mother cried and said, "If God will bring Ma'ruf back, we will follow whatever religion he adopts." A few years later, he returned to his mother. The mother said, "O my son, what religion do you follow?"

"I embraced Islam," he replied. Her mother immediately made the declaration of faith, "I bear witness that there is no God but Allah and I bear witness that Muhammad is the messenger of Allah." My mother embraced Islam, followed by the rest of the family.

Ahmad ibn al-Fath said:

In a dream I saw Bisyr ibn al-Hârits sitting in a garden eating a dish. I asked him: "O Abû Nashr, what did God do to you?" He replied: "He forgave me. He also gave me Paradise and everything in it. Allah told me, 'Eat all its fruits and drink from all its streams. Enjoy all its contents as you used to deprive yourself of various desires in the world."

I asked again, "Where is your brother Ahmad ibn Hanbal?"

He replied, "He is standing at the door of heaven, interceding for the Ahl al-Sunnah who hold that the Quran is the word of Allah, not a creature."

Never worship at the graves since this is polytheism, but pray to Allah alone for the dead person who needs your prayers to raise his status in the sight of Allah.

4

O my negligent brothers, come to your senses! O addicts of sin, give it up and come to your senses! By Allah, is there any human being worse than a propagator of lust? Who is more lost than one who sells the Hereafter for the world? Why does negligence rule your hearts? Why do you let ignorance cover your disgrace? Don't you see the pain of death scattered around you, its arrival so evident, its signal has arrived, its map scorching the grounds, its arrow penetrating you, and its destiny piercing your crown? Until when? Until when? Why do you still turn away and remain silent?

Do you want to live forever? Impossible, for God's sake. Death is always lurking. No one escapes, whether father or son. Therefore, truly serve God. Abandon all sins, may He protect you.

Muhammad ibn Quddâmah relates:

Bisyr ibn al-Hârits met a man who was drunk. The man embraced him saying, "O Abû Nashr." He let the man embrace him until he was satisfied. When the man left, Bisyr's eyes filled with tears. He said, "One who loves another because he thinks there is good in him may be saved, while the beloved does not know his own fate."

Then he stood in front of the owner of the fruit. He stared for a long time. I asked, "O Abû Nashr, is there any fruit that you want?" He replied, "No. I was just thinking, if He gives to the disobedient, what more to those who obey Him. What kind of food and drink will He give him in Paradise?"

O my brother, how long will the negligent sleep? Does not the alternation of night and day awaken him? Where are the dwellers of palaces? By God, death has circled above and stalked them like a pigeon.

Beings are impermanent when the glue-bar notes have been folded and the pen has dried.

Let me weep and wail in a torrent of tears

Let me wail for fear that my weak self will perish.

Where shall I take refuge and where shall I go?

Who can help me when I am called to sin?

How long the sorrow and anguish when in Hell

All the ugliness seems so real

The balance sheet is near and the fire has been lit

With my best wishes to Him, may God be pleased to grant me bounty

And with His mercy enter me into paradise

The Messenger of Allah (peace be upon him) said, "On the Day of Judgment, a person will be brought who has accumulated wealth from lawful means and spent it on lawful means. He will be called, 'Stand up to be judged!' He will be judged for every bit of his wealth; where it was earned and what it was spent on." The Prophet (peace be upon him) continued, "O man, what have you done with the world? Its lawful is to be judged and its unlawful is to be tortured."

Do not feel secure with the good of the world

The good of the world is a source of corruption

Do not rejoice in the wealth you get

It contains the opposite of what is desired.

A wise man tells a story:

On the eve of his death, Abû Yazid al-Busthâmî would cry and then laugh. Shortly after Abu Yazid died, someone dreamed of meeting him. Abu Yazid was asked, "Why did you cry and then laugh before dying?" He replied, "When I was dying, the cursed devil came to me saying, 'O Abu Yazid, you have taken off my ring.' I cried to Allah. Then an angel descended from the sky and said, "O Abu Yazîd, God says to you: "Do not be afraid and do not be sad! Be happy with paradise!" I laughed and left the world."

I stood with tears in my eyes

My heart was troubled for fear of the verdict

Every guilty one perishes by his sin

He is abject, sad, closed, and full of remorse

O Lord, my sins are so great

You know what I am complaining about

You are the Most Compassionate, the Most Merciful, and the Almighty

Most Gracious, Most Forgiving, and Most Merciful.

O my brother, how many days have you spent delaying repentance. How many causes made you neglect your duty. How often have your ears heard without fear of threats.

On the eve of his death, Jabir ibn Zayd was asked, "What is it that you desire?" "To see the face of al-Hasan," he replied. Hearing this, al-Hasan immediately came to Jâbir and asked, "O Jâbir, what is your condition?" He replied, "I feel that Allah's decree cannot be denied. O Abu Sa'id tell me a hadith that you heard from the Messenger of Allah." Al-Hasan said: "O Jâbir, the Messenger of Allah said: 'A believer is always in good standing with God. If he repents, Allah accepts him, if he apologizes, Allah forgives him, and if he asks for forgiveness, Allah forgives him. The sign of all this is the cold that he feels in his heart before the soul comes out.'" Jâbir exclaimed, "Allahu Akbar! I feel cold in my heart." He then prayed, "O Allah, I hope for Your reward. Make my hope a reality and remove my anxiety and fear!" He then said *shahada* and passed away. May Allah be pleased with him.

It is said that Dâwûd al-Thâ'î repented because he, while passing by the cemetery, heard the soft humming of cries from the grave.

5

O my brother, bind the soul with control, keep the heart away from sin, and read the lesson sheet with the tongue of understanding! O heedless of death and foresight, O brave in deeds! Wake up, O sleeper! How many years you have wasted. The whole world has become your bed. The most beautiful things are only unreal dreams. Old, but your mind is like a child's. Don't you see, the conqueror of the lust is the true brave. Negligence has peaked and disaster is approaching. Inna lillah wa inna ilayhi râji'ûn.

Once the Prophet 'Îsâ a.s. passed by a village and found all its inhabitants dead. scattered on the ground. He was shocked and said, "O disciples, they died in a state of anger and wrath. Had they died in a state of contentment with Allah, they would have buried each other." The disciples asked Jesus (peace be upon him), "O servant of Allah, we want to know their news and their condition." Prophet 'Îsâ a.s. then prayed to Allah and received a revelation: "When the night comes, call them! They will answer your call."

When night fell, Prophet 'Îsâ a.s. climbed to a high place and called out, "O our people!" It turned out that someone among them replied, "Yes, we accept your call, O Prophet of Allah." Îsâ a.s. asked, "How are you?" The man replied, "O servant of Allah, we were fine before, but then we had a disaster."
"How did it happen?"
"We were too much in love with the world, obeying the sinners, not commanding good, and not preventing evil."

"How do you love the world?"

"Like a child who loves his mother. If the mother comes, the child is very happy, and if she leaves, he is sad and cries."

"O *Fulan*, why do others not respond to my call?"

"They are bound with the bridles of hell by hard and harsh angels."

"How, then, can you fulfill my message?"

"I am not among them but am in their midst. When doom fell upon them, it fell upon me as well. Now I am hanging on the edge of the abyss of hell. I do not know whether I will survive or fall."

May Allah protect us from hell. O you who spend your life in transgression, weep for the calamity that has befallen you! It may be that your eng- is rejected. O one whose age has passed while the past does not return, a number of exhortations as guidance you have received, gray hair has told you that you will die, and the tongue of instruction calls out, "O man, you are really striving towards God."

When the time of relationship and favor has passed you ask for what has passed back

Have I not visited and offered to bind?

Your white hairs are so bright from all sides.

O my brother, it is time to return, ask for forgiveness, and forsake sin.

"Whoever reaches the age of forty years, while his goodness does not outweigh its badness, prepare for hell."

I come to you in hope, O Lord

Take away, as you see it, the ugliness of my condition

I have disobeyed you with my foolishness

The disgrace of sin has never crossed my mind

To whom else do I turn but to you, the Lord of all worlds?
Ruler of all the worlds, my Lord?

Woe is me! If only my mother had not given birth to me and
in the darkness of the night I had not disobeyed You

Here I am, Your guilty servant O Most High God, standing
at Your door

If You wish to punish me, O Lord, doom and punishment
are indeed fitting for me.

If You forgive me, Your forgiveness I truly hope for

With Your forgiveness, my bad state will become good.

Allah swt. says, "O My servant, do you not know that I
created the world as a place of burden and test? Do you not
know that I only give a good and honorable position to those
who repent to Me from sins and mistakes? Why do you not
approach My door, do not expect My bounty and reward,
and do not fear My punishment and wrath?"

O you who are so negligent and ignorant, take heed of God's
love and bounty upon you!

Remove the burden of sin on your back with repentance!

Come with your heart to the Knower of all hidden things!

Wash your face with tears!

Put on the garment of humility and submission!

I committed many sins until I met humiliation

My tears flowed so much I cursed the heart that had realized

To whom will I complain if not to the Master, the Ruler of all servants?

Your mercy, O Sustainer of the Throne, is certainly preferable.

6

Brother, wake up from your negligence, for negligence is a long deep sleep. Get ready for your hereafter, for this world is only a place to stop by and take a nap.

In a narration it is mentioned that Allah (the Most High) revealed to one of His prophets, "O My prophet, how different is the one who disobeys My commands from the one who spends his age in constant contact with Me, remembers Me, is at My door, and wets his cheeks for Me. How ashamed is he who sins and how sorry is he who does not do good."

Be alone if you want to get closer

Leave humans far away there

Try to break all ties in life

by penetrating the mortal veil.

It is narrated that the Prophet (peace and blessings of Allah be upon him) said, "O my companions, do you know who a bankrupt is?" They replied, "O Messenger of Allah, a bankrupt, according to us, is one who has no dinars and dirhams at all." He said, "No, that is not it. The bankrupt is the one who comes on the Day of Judgment with prayer, fasting, zakat, and alms, but he has reviled so-and-so, wronged so-and-so, eaten so-and-so's wealth, and shed so-and-so's blood. Therefore, he must pay "compensation" to them with his wealth. It turned out that before his obligation was paid, his kindness had already been exhausted. Finally, their faults and sins were taken and credited to him, and he was thrown into hell. This is the one who is bankrupt."" May Allah (the Most High) protect us from this.

A pious man told me:

I went to the mosque to see Ibrâhîm ibn Adham, but he was not there. Someone told me that Ibrâhîm had left the mosque. I went out to look for him. It turned out that he was sleeping in the middle of the valley under the hot sun. A large snake was coiled above his head. It was waving a sprig of jasmine in its mouth to keep the flies away from Ibrâhîm. I was astonished to see it. Suddenly the snake was made to speak by God Who makes all things speak. The snake said, "What are you astonished at?" I replied, "I am astonished and amazed by your actions and even more so by your ability to speak, even though you are an enemy of man." "By Allah, Allah has only made us enemies to those who disobey, while we are subject to obedient servants," replied the snake.

My deeds are bad, while my hope is good

My Lord is Oft-Forgiving and Most-Giving

You challenge your Lord, O transgressor but fearful of the neighbor because of his intelligence

I still commit sins, while gray hairs have come

By Allah, O self, is this good?

Rise up to Him, O servant, and hope

Say to Him, "O Bestower of bounty"

Say, "O Fountain of hope If it is not You who forgives me, who else?

Al-Hasan al-Basri was about to deliver a message. People were crowding to get close to him. He then came to them and said, "O brothers, you are crowding to get close to me, and how will you be on the Day of Judgment when the assembly of the pious is brought near and the assembly of the unjust is kept far away, and the one carrying a light load is called, 'Pass!' and the one carrying a heavy load is called, 'Stop!'? Will I be stopped with the group carrying heavy loads or allowed to pass with the group carrying light loads?" Al-Hasan then wept and became unconscious. The people around him were also crying.

After a while, he called out again:

O my brothers, do you not weep for fear of hell? Know, Allah will save the one who cries for fear of hell when all creatures are drawn to hell with shackles and chains.

O my brothers, do you not weep out of longing for Allah?

Know that the one who cries out of longing for Allah will not be prevented from seeing Him on the Day of Judgment when His mercy peaks, His forgiveness appears, and His wrath against the wrongdoers intensifies.

O my brothers, will you not weep over the calamity of thirst on the Day of Judgment? At that time all creatures will be gathered in a state of thirst, and they will not find any water except the lake of the Prophet Muhammad (peace be upon him). Some people may drink, but others are prevented (those who invent new things such as those who invented the celebration of the Prophet's birthday will be prevented unless they repent and believe like the Salaf believed). The one who cries over the calamity of thirst on the Day of Judgment will be given a drink by Allah from the spring of Paradise Firdaus.

How unfortunate if I cannot drink from the pool of the Prophet when thirsty on the Day of Judgment.

He then cried and said:

By Allah, one day I passed by a woman who worshipped diligently. She pleaded, "O Lord, I am tired of living because of your longing and expectation." I asked, "O Fulanah, are you sure of your deeds?" She replied, "My love for Him and my desire to meet Him make me content. Will He torture me when I love Him?"

Suddenly a small child from my family crossed my path. I immediately grabbed the child, hugged him, and kissed him. The woman asked, "Do you love this child?" "Yes," I replied. Hearing my answer, she cried and said, "If all people knew what they would face tomorrow, they would not have a good time, will not be at ease and will not enjoy even a little of this world."

A moment later, the woman's son, Dhaygham, arrived. She asked, "O Dhaygham, do you think we will meet or be separated on the Day of Judgment?" The child immediately cried out. I guess his heart was hurt and sad. He then fell unconscious. The woman cried for him and I cried too.

When the child woke up, the woman called out to him, "O Dhaygham!" "Yes, Mother," he replied. "Do you wish to die?" his mother asked. "Yes," he replied. The mother again asked, "Why, O my son?" He replied, "To return to the One who is better than you, that is the Merciful Lord. I want to return to the One who fed me in the darkness of your womb and brought me out of the narrowness of the exit of the womb. If He had wanted to, He could have killed me on the way out of the narrow birth canal and you would have died in pain. But, in His mercy, He made it easy for me and for you. Have you not heard Allah's words: 'Tell My servants that I am the Most Forgiving and the Most Merciful, and that My punishment is a very painful punishment."

The child then cried and exclaimed, "Reproach me if I am not saved from the punishment of Allah." He continued to cry until he became unconscious and fell to the ground.

The mother approached and held him. It turned out that he was dead. The woman burst into tears and said, "O Dhaygham, O one who died for the love of Allah." She continued to cry until she fell to the ground. I moved her body, and she was dead. May the mercy of Allah Almighty be upon them and upon all of us.

7

O my brother, the world is a murderous poison, while the soul is oblivious to its deceptions. How many views are sweet in the world, while the bitterness in the Hereafter is unbearable. O man, your heart is fragile, your sight is blurred, your eyes are loose, your tongue nets sins, and your body is weary of scavenging the debris of the world. How many despicable views have led to slipped feet.

I blamed my heart when I saw the thinness of my body

My heart blamed my eyes, saying, "You are my messenger."

My eyes replied, "You are my guide."

Finally I said, "Stop! Do you want to kill me?"

The Prophet 'Îsâ a.s. said, "The sight of the eyes plants lust in the heart."

Ibrâhîm chanted:

If anyone was given enemies and envy, I was given eyes and a heart.

Ibn 'Abbâs r.a. relates that the Messenger of Allah was visited by a man covered with blood. The Messenger of Allah asked, "What happened to you?" The man replied, "I passed in front of a woman. I kept staring at her, so I hit the wall. This is how it happened." The Prophet (peace and blessings of Allah be upon him) said, "Whenever Allah wills good for someone, He hastens his punishment in this world."

Abû Ya'qûb al-Nahrajûri narrates:

While circumambulating, I heard a one-eyed man praying, "I seek refuge with You from You." I asked, "Why do you pray like that?" He replied, "I have been a neighbor for fifty years. One day I was looking at someone who I thought was beautiful. Suddenly a hard slap hit me in the eye and my blood ran cold. 'Ouch,' I said. Shortly after, another slap came. After that, there was a voice: 'If you do it again, I will increase it.'"

Let me call out to the Most High God when the night lowers its curtain on me I look to You with humility for You,

You are the God who never changes

All praise, glory, and greatness belong to You

You are the God who is always praiseworthy, gracious, great, and glorious

You made mankind and you brought bones to life

You created generation after generation, age after age

Your greatness is so great and Your deeds are so glorious

Your bounty is abundant and Your bounty is great

Your bounty is abundant for every servant who asks

You are the Most Loving and Forgiving of sins

You cover disgrace and You forgive the guilty fools

You demand little, while You give abundantly in bounty and grace

Your treasury of generosity is never ending, encompassing the humble and the generous.

A wise man told me a story:

We traveled with a group from Iraq to Makkah and Madinah. Among us was a man, an Iraqi man whose yellow body had a yellowish-red color. The blood on his face seemed to have disappeared because of his diligent worship. He wore worn-out clothes full of patches. His hands held a stick and supplies.

The abid and zahid was Uways al-Qarni. The companions were uncomfortable with his appearance. They said to him, "You seem to be a servant." "Yes," he replied. "It looks like you are a misbehaving servant who has run away from your master." "Yes," he replied. They continued, "How do you feel after running away from your master? How are you doing? Wouldn't you not be like this if you stayed with him? You are a misbehaving and guilty servant." Uways responded, "Yes, I am indeed a bad servant. The best employer is my Master, yet I have done so much wrong. Had I obeyed Him and sought His pleasure, I would not be like this." He then cried until he almost died.

Seeing him like that, people felt sorry for him. They thought that he was referring to his earthly employer, when in fact he was referring to Allah Rabul-alamin. Someone advised, "Don't be afraid, I will ask for a guarantee of safety from your employer. Go back and ask for forgiveness!" Uways said, "I will return to Him and hope for what is with Him."

Uways and others traveled together with great enthusiasm. When night fell, they stopped at a field. It was a cold night and raining heavily. They took shelter in their vehicles and tents, except Uways. He stayed in the clearing and did not get a ride anywhere. He had made a promise to himself not to ask anything from the creatures. He asked only Allah Swt. for all his needs. So cold was the air that his whole body shivered. He finally froze to death in the middle of the night. In the morning, when the group was about to leave, they called out to Uways, "Get up! The people are leaving." As Uways did not respond, the nearest man came and moved his body. He found him dead. "O group, this servant who ran away from his master is dead," he exclaimed, "You should not leave before burying him."

They asked, "Why is that?" A pious man among them explained, "He was a repentant servant who wanted to return to his master. He regrets what he has done. May Allah benefit us through him. He has accepted his repentance. We fear prosecution if we leave him alone. You must be patient until we finish digging the graves and burying them."
Some of them said, "There is no water here." Others said, "Ask the guide!" The guide said, "It will take an hour to reach the water. Send one person with me, I will bring you water."

The guide picked up a bucket. Not far into the walk, he suddenly saw a pool of water. "How strange, I've never seen this pond before. As far as I know, there is no water around here," he said.

He quickly returned to the group and said, "Your needs have been met. You just need to prepare firewood." They gathered firewood to heat the water. When they went to the pond to fetch water, they found it was already hot. They were even more astonished. "This servant must have some specialty," they concluded.

They began to dig his grave. It turned out that the soil was very soft and gave off a musk-like fragrance. They had never smelled such a fragrance. What they saw was only soil, but the soil was so fragrant like musk.

They then set up camp and placed Uways' body inside. They competed to shroud Uways. Each one said, "I will shroud him." Finally, they agreed that everyone was welcome to contribute a shroud for him.

They took ink and paper to write down the characteristics of Uways. They thought, "When we get to Madinah, God willing, hopefully someone will recognize him there." They put the note in the place of the goods.

When Uways was washed and about to be shrouded, the ba ju attached to his body was uncovered. It turned out that he had been shrouded in a cloth from heaven. This was the first time they had all witnessed such a thing. They found amber on the shroud. The fragrance spread in all directions. On his forehead and feet there was a stamp of musk.

They said, "La hawla wa la quwwata illâ billah al-'aliyy al-'azhim. Allah swt. has shrouded him perfectly so that he does not need a human shroud. May Allah swt. grant us paradise and bless us on account of this righteous servant."

They were very sorry that they had abandoned him to freeze to death that night.

They then took him for prayer and burial. When they said takbir, they heard the sound of takbir from all corners of heaven and earth. Their hearts and eyes felt like they were going to fall out. They were so scared, they didn't know how to pray for him. They were even more afraid when they heard a voice from above. After that, they took him to be buried. His body was so light as if it were flying. They buried him and left his grave with a feeling of wonder and amazement.

When they reached the mosque, they informed them of the above incident and the description of the man. It turned out that the people there recognized him. The mosque was filled with weeping. Had it not been for this information, no one would have known of his death and grave, for Uways always hid and avoided people. May Allah swt. benefit us from this story and make us worship Him alone.

8

O my brother, how long will this negligence continue, while you see untimely deaths around you? Promise to fill your days with goodness and mend your broken deeds! Always be aware of the coming of death! The call for departure has sounded and the accounting awaits, but you are still playing with death. Oh, how heavy is this burden, while how poor are the companions who accompany. How little provisions, while how far the journey.

O doomsayer who is deceived by the lies of wishful thinking and is out of the truth! You are only pretending to be on the truth.

O unemployed person, how long will you delay repentance, when there is no forgiveness before repentance? Until when will you continue to be lulled and deceived? O loser, the months of goodness are over, while you are still counting the months. Will you be accepted or rejected? Are you connected or have you been cut off? Will you ride a special animal or will you be pulled? Are you a resident of Hell or Paradise? By Allah, truly fortunate is the one who is light of burden and truly miserable is the one who is guilty. Only to Allah is the return of all affairs.

Why, I see, do you persevere in sin? Do you feel safe from the severity of the account? Do not be negligent, it seems your day has come. It may be that your age is near and your beloved will soon dig your grave.

Death came to warn the neighbors.

They brought the person who used to bathe and bathe you as a naked corpse

After being bathed, you were given the clothes of death

To carry your bed, called the brothers

Your family came to take you to say goodbye

For you they shed tears of lies

Fear God, for the servant who fears will dwell in heaven with His full pleasure

A paradise of everlasting pleasure with fragrant scents everywhere.

As for the disobedient, hell

Fire burns the face and the whole body

We cry and we deserve to cry so that

IIe will not punish us for our sins.

The Prophet (peace and blessings of Allah be upon him) said:

When man faces death, Allah sends five angels. The first angel comes when the soul is in the throat. This angel calls out, "O man, where is your strong body? How weak it is now! Where is your eloquent tongue? How weak it is now! Where are your family and relatives? How alone you are now!"

The second angel came when his soul was grasped and his shroud was spread. This angel calls out, "O people, where is the wealth that you prepared for poverty? Where is the prosperity that you have prepared for destruction? Where is the pleasure that you have prepared for loneliness?"

The third angel came when he was brought in poverty. This angel called out, "O man, today you are going on a long journey. This journey is farther than all your previous journeys. Now you will meet a people whom you have never met and will be able to meet them. Enter into a narrow place that you have never entered. Blessed are you if you gain Allah's favor. Woe to you if you return with the wrath of Allah."

The fourth angel came when he was in the grave. This angel called out, "O man, yesterday you walked on it, but now you lie in it. Yesterday you laughed over it, while now you weep in it. Yesterday you sinned over it, but now you regret in it. The fifth angel came when he was covered with earth, and family, neighbors, and friends had moved away. This angel calls out, "O man, they have buried you and left you. Even if they remain with you, they cannot benefit you. You have accumulated wealth and left it for others. Now you are headed for a high heaven or a hot hell."

A young worshipper prayed, "O Lord, I disobey you when strong and obey you when weak. I angered You when I was strong and served You when I was poor. O Lord, will You accept me despite my humiliation or reject me for sin?"

He then fell unconscious and cut his forehead.

His mother rushed over and embraced him. She rubbed his forehead as she sobbed, "Oh, my eye-flavorer in this world and the fruit of my heart in the next, speak, son, to your lonely mother! Answer your old mother!"

The young man came to his senses and held his chest, while his spirit rose and fell. Tears ran down his cheeks and beard. He said to his mother, "O mother, this is the moment you warned me about. This is the death you warned me about. This is the terrible death and the fall of all burdens. What a loss of days missed. How restless to face the long days that I am unprepared for. Oh mother, I fear a long stay in the prison of hell. How sad I would be if thrown into hell. How wretched I would be if I fell into hell. Mother, please do what I am about to say to you!"

His mother replied, "O my son, I am willing to be your ransom. What do you want?" He said, "Put my cheek on the ground and step on it so that I may taste the humiliation of this world and the pleasure of God. May He love me and save me from the blazing hell."

The mother immediately carried out her son's request. As soon as his cheek pressed against the ground, her tears were flowing profusely. When the mother stepped on his cheeks with both feet, he said softly, "This is the reward of one who sins and disobeys. This is the reward of those who do wrong and evil. This is the reward of one who does not stand at

God's door. This is the reward of one who does not feel the presence of the Most High and Glorious God."

He died on the spot. In a dream, his mother saw him with a beautiful face like the moon. The mother asked, "O my son, what has God done for you?" "He elevated my rank and placed me near the Prophet Muhammad, peace be upon him," he replied. His mother asked him again, "O my son, what do you mean by the words I heard at the time of your death?" He replied, "O mother, a voice whispered to me, 'O 'Imrân, answer the caller of God!' I answered him and welcomed the call of God." May Allah have mercy on him.

9

O my brother, this journey is bound to happen. Why do we want to live in this land that is not our home? Year after year is just a terminal. Month after month is just a stage. Day after day is just a round. Breaths are steps. Disobedience is the breaker. Gain is heaven and loss is hell.

We are destined to reach the eternal place through six stages of the journey. The first journey is from the ground to the collarbone. The second journey is from the collarbone to the womb. The third journey is from the womb to the world. The fourth journey is from the world to the grave. The fifth journey from the grave to the place of assembly (on the Day of Resurrection). The sixth journey is from place of assembly to the eternal land, heaven or hell. We have passed half the journey. What remains is the hardest.

O screamer when suffering, let God manage, so that you can rest.

You cry and lament a lot but forget the bad deeds you have done.

If you return to Him with all your heart, He will release all your distress and anguish.

O my brother, beware of the world.

The rope of the world must be cut off.

Be wise; remember, you will die.

Ibn al-Mubarak said:

I once came to Makkah during a long drought. People were praying istisqa prayer (prayer for rain) at Masjid-al-haram. At the door of Banu Shaybah, I prayed with them. Suddenly there was a black slave wearing two pieces of coarse cloth. One was used as a sarong and the other was worn as a sling on the shoulder. He took his place beside me. I heard him pray, "O Lord, this face has aged with many sins and bad deeds. You deprive us of the rain as a warning. I beseech you, O Most Merciful. O One known only for good, grant them rain this very moment!"

He continued to pray, "Give them rain right now!" until the sky filled with clouds and the rain fell like a spill. He then sat down and glorified Allah. I cried until he got up. When he left, I followed him to find out where he lived.

After that, I went to al-Fudhayl ibn 'Iyadh. He asked, "Why do you look sad?" I said, "There is another person who has preceded us to Him until He appointed him as a guardian." He asked, "What do you mean?" I told him about that person. Upon hearing my story, al-Fudhayl cried out and fell down. He said, "O Ibn al-Mubarak, take me to him!" Our time is very short, but I will try," I said.

The next day, after the dawn prayer, I went to his residence. An old man was sitting at the door of the house I was going to. When he saw me, he recognized me. "Welcome, O Abû 'Abd al-Rahmân. What is the need?" he greeted. I replied, "A slave." He called one of his slaves, and said, "The work of this slave is always good. I will give him to you." "No, he is not the one I am looking for," I said. He then took out one slave after another until finally the slave appeared. Seeing him, my tears welled up. He asked, "Is this he?" "Yes," I replied. "I will not sell he," said the grandfather. "Why?" I asked. He replied, "He brings me blessings. I have never had any calamity or disaster since he has been with me here." I asked, "How does he earn his food?" "He earns approximately one-sixth of a dirham from spinning rope. He eats if he sells the rope. If not, he lays around all day."

Other slaves related that he did not sleep through the night and was always alone. He was more preoccupied with himself. My heart loved him even more.

After going to see al-Fudhayl ibn 'lyâdh and Sufyân al-Tsawrî with an unfulfilled desire, I returned to grandfather, the slave owner. I continued to plead with him until finally he said, "Your earnestness melted my heart. Please take him as you wish."

I bought him and immediately took him to al-Fudhayl's house. On the way, he suddenly said, "O master!"

"Labbayka!" I replied.

"Do not say: labbayka. The servant is more worthy of saying that than the master."

"What is the matter, O my beloved?"

"My body is so weak that I cannot serve. You could have taken another, better slave. He has offered a slave who is stronger and more manly than I am."

"I will not make you work. I am buying you for my son."

Hearing that, he burst into tears. "Why are you crying?" I asked.

"You did this after seeing some of my relationship with Allah Swt. Otherwise, why did you choose me among my many friends?"

"Is that all?"

"By Allah, I would not have asked if you had told me."

"With the fulfillment of your prayer."

"I consider you to be -insha Allah- a righteous person. Allah swt. has the best servants among His creatures. He does not reveal their state except to His beloved servants and does not reveal to them except those whom He pleases."

He then said, "What if we stop for a moment? There are some rak'ahs that I did not do last night." "The house of al-Fudhayl is near," I said. He insisted, "No. I would rather be here. The command of Allah Almighty should not be delayed." He then went to the mosque and prayed. After the prayer, he turned to me and said, "O Abû 'Abd al-Rahmân, do you have a need?"

"Why?"

"Because, I want to go."

"Where to?"

"To the hereafter."

"No! I want to benefit from you."

"Life is beautiful only when I have a relationship with God. If you know my relationship with Him, others will know it too. I don't want that myself."

He then prostrated himself and prayed, "O God, take my life right now!" When I approached him, it was obvious that he had passed away. By Allah, I was sad every time I remembered him. The world and my deeds became very low in my sight. May Allah have mercy on him and on all of us.

10

O man, you often dress in the garb of *abid* (worshipper of Allah) and *Zahid* (being conscious of Allah), while your heart is negligent. Your outward appearance is clean, but your inner being is dirty, polluted by wishful thinking. True love cannot reside in those who love wealth. Had there been no merit in the struggle, they would not have been called figures.

O dead-hearted one, your promise in this world is true, while in the hereafter it is impossible. If you did not hasten in your youth, hasten in your old age! After gray hair, there is no more banter and playfulness. It is strange that when you are old, you still slip. You have wasted your youth in carelessness. You are filled with lamentation. Had you known the record of your deeds, you would have cried all night.

Someone asked Dzû al-Nûn al-Mishrî r.a., "O Shaykh, what should I do? Every time I stand at one of God's doors, I am turned away by calamities and trials." He replied, "O my brother, stand at the door of your Lord like a child before his mother. Whenever his mother beats him, he kneels at her feet. Whenever she chased him away, he drew closer. He continues to do so until the mother embraces him."

It is narrated that the Prophet 'Îsâ a.s. traveled the world. He said, "My mount is my legs. My clothing is hair. My motto is fear of God. My perfume is grass. My food is wheat bread. My shade is the darkness of the night. My house is the place where I dwell. All that, for a man who is bound to die, is plenty."

Al-Shiblî r.a. relates the story of his encounter with a Bedouin who served the worshippers of Allah in Makkah. When the reason was asked, the Bedouin told him:

I live in the countryside. One day I saw a young boy with no feet and no head covering. He also had no provisions, except a drink holder, and a stick. I intended, "I will visit that young man. If he is hungry, I will feed him. If he is thirsty, I will give him a drink." I quickly approached him until there was only a cubit between me and him. He moved away and suddenly disappeared from my sight. "This must be the devil," I thought. Immediately he replied, "No, it's not."

"O Fulan! By Allah Who sent Muhammad (peace be upon him) with the truth, will you not come to me?"

"O young man, you are only making myself and yourself tired." "I see you are alone. Therefore, I want to help you."

"How can one who is with Allah alone?"
"I see you have no provisions either."
"If hungry, my provision is the remembrance of Him. If thirsty, my desire is to witness Him."

Since then I have been serving the poor in the hope of meeting a person of Tawheed (worshipping Allah alone and asking help from Him alone) like him.

O people, how long will you hear the news of the pious but not follow in their footsteps? Befriend the *Salafis (Ahle-Hadeeth)*, may you be guided on their path! Weep for your distance, O expelled one! People like you deserve to weep and lament. Ask for forgiveness, O outcast! With humility, you will be happy. Recite the following stanza with the tongue of humility, regret, and sorrow:

How many people reproach, and yet they themselves do

How many weaknesses do not want to be moved by the strong.

How often have I uttered false words

Speech is useless if it is not accompanied by deeds.

Real deeds.

What a wonder! How often have I rebuked the alienated, but the rebuke has no benefit. How often have I called out to the heedless, but you have not listened. How often have I knocked on your heart, but you did not care. Woe to you, O owner of eyes that never shed a tear! Among the signs of inattention is a heart that is never solemn. Your heart is immersed in the love of something mortal. You are even busy collecting *haram* treasures. O negligent one, the treasures you have accumulated will be judged and you will leave them with those who cannot benefit you, while you yourself are in the valley of negligence. You hear people saying, "So-and-so has gone away and will never return."

'Ali ibn Abi Shâlih relates:

While traveling around Mount Lukkam in search of *Salafis* and *Ahle-Hadeeth* (the true Abids and Zahids), I saw a man wearing a patched shirt. He was sitting on a rock looking down. I asked, "O Shaykh, what are you doing here?" "I am looking and observing," he replied.

"All I see in front of you is a rock. What is it that you are looking at and observing?" "I am looking at the trajectory of the heart and observing the God's commands. You have distracted me from God."

"Say something that is beneficial to me!"

"Whoever is always at His door, will be diligent in his service. Whoever remembers a lot of sins, regrets a lot. Whoever is content with God, will not fear nothingness."

He then left me. May Allah swt. be pleased with him.

11

O you who so deftly seek the world, when will your search end? Seeking the Hereafter, you are sluggish; when will you learn? How strange! You are eagerly seeking something short-lived, while there are many intruders on the way. Age is a mandate. You spend youth in betrayal, old age in unemployment, and old age in crying: "I have lived long." When is a traitor lucky with what he buys or sells? You are healthy when pursuing the world, but sick when pursuing the hereafter. How often have you turned away from the path of piety, O person who lives at the bottom of the abyss. O owner of the nights of forgetfulness, gray hair has appeared. Join the repentant before you are cut off with the rest! "Nothing is hidden in the heavens and the earth but it is found in the Book of the Unseen (al-lauh al-mahfuzh)."

If I am not patient with the One I love and if I cannot communicate, what can I do?

Will I abandon Him, while this heart is held captive by the heartfelt love that is poured out to Him?

Would I allow reproaches about Him, while this love is raging?

What I hear can't really be replaced by reproach

Will I forget, while longing makes me remember always or will I cover up what is revealed by tears?

My heart condemns me when my love for Him increases I don't care about the others, no matter what obstacles come my way

When His love increases for me, I complain to Him

In every complaint, He alone is my helper.

I see the time passing by moment by moment at a time when I have not obtained all my desires

If I feel narrow with what I have met everything that is narrow becomes broad in love.

"Teach me something by which Allah will benefit me."

"Serve your Lord with longing to meet Him."

"O Lord, how long will you leave me in a land where I do not find friends who can help me overcome calamities?"

If a servant's sickness is love for his Lord, what else can be expected to cure it.

O my brother, if God expels you from His door, to which door will you return? Which way will you go? Which direction will you go? Do not leave the door of your Lord, may you return with fruit!

The pleasure of the hearts of the wise is dhikr (remembrance of Allah). The Dhikr should be based on the prayers of remembrance that are authentic and which were taught by the Prophet (peace and blessings of Allah be upon him).

Conclusion

Our safety lies in avoiding sins and doing all the obligatory actions that Allah has commanded. We should join the Ahle-Sunnah Wal Jamaat and stick to the Jamaat and the mainstream scholars who have studied from Salafi and Ahle-Hadeeth institutions and who have the aqeedah of the Salaf-us-Saliheen.

Allah guide us all to the straight way and to Your pleasure.

Ameen!